Polish Proverbs

Collected by Joanne Asala

Wycinanki by Alice Wadowski-Bak

Penfield
Press

Dedicated to the memory of my grandmother
Emma Kuyat Dawson.

— *Joanne Asala*

Wycinanki dedicated to my son Captain Gregory Bak and
his new bride, Rebecca.

— *Alice Wadowski-Bak*

Cover Art: Designed by Alice Wadowski-Bak.
Graphic Design: Robyn Loughran.
Edited by: Dorothy Papich Crum, Marlene Jorgensen Perrin,
Krystyna Gutt, Eva M. Boicourt, Georgia Heald and
Joan Liffring-Zug.

Books by Mail
Polish Proverbs
Czech Proverbs
$10.95 each, postpaid to one address. Prices subject to change.

For a complete catalog of titles please send $2.00 to:
Penfield Press
215 Brown Street
Iowa City, IA 52245

There is a proverb for everything.

Na wszystko jest przysłowie.

About the Author

Joanne Asala is a writer and editor dedicated to the preservation of folklore and traditional customs. Of Polish and Finnish descent, she grew up in Bloomingdale, Illinois, and earned an English degree from the University of Iowa with an emphasis in Medieval literature. Joanne has traveled extensively through Eastern and Western Europe gathering folktales, proverbs and traditional recipes. Her titles for Penfield Press include *Fairy Tales of the Slav Peasants and Herdsmen* and *Czech Proverbs*. She currently lives in Chicago, near the neighborhood known as "Little Poland," an area of approximately 40 blocks of Polish-American businesses serving Polish immigrants and their descendants.

About the Artist

Alice Wadowski-Bak learned the art of wycinanki from Polish artists while on a cultural exchange to Poland with the United States Information Agency's exhibit tour "Graphic Arts, U.S.A."

Born and raised in Niagara Falls, New York, she studied art at Syracuse University and graduated from the University of Buffalo with a Bachelor of Fine Arts degree. She earned her Master's degree from Niagara University.

Alice has worked as a textile designer, a book and magazine illustrator in New York City, and as a teacher of art and folk art at several colleges. She works in Niagara Falls and has two grown sons, Gregory and Kenneth, who continue to inspire her.

She has exhibited her art and paintings extensively and her work is in numerous private collections.

Select List of Consulted Sources:

Adalberg, S. *Polish Proverbs*. Warsaw. 1889–94.

Bauer-Czarnomski, Francis. *Proverbs in Polish and English*. London. 1920.

Bechtel, John H. *Proverbs, Maxims and Phrases Drawn From Many Lands*. London. 1906.

Bohn, H. G. *A Polyglot of Foreign Proverbs*. London. 1857.

Bohn, H. G. *A Handbook of Proverbs*. London. 1855.

Bystrom, Professor Jan. *A Treatise on Polish Proverbs*. 1913.

Christy, Robert. *Proverbs, Maxims and Phrases*. New York. 1887. Reprint. Norwood, Pennsylvania. 1977.

Conklin, George. *The World's Best Proverbs*. Philadelphia. 1906.

Dennys, E.M. *Proverbs and Quotations of Many Lands*. London. 1890.

Hulme, F. Edward. *Proverb Lore*. London: Elliot Stock, 1902. Reprint. Detroit: Gale Research Company, 1968.

Johnson, H. *Proverbs*. New York. 1885.

Kelly, Walter K. *Proverbs of all Nations*. London. 1859.

Kelly, Walter K. *A Collection of the Proverbs of All Nations*. Andover. 1879. Reprint: Folcroft Library Editions.

King, W.F.H. *Classical and Foreign Quotations*. London. 1889.

Middlemore, James. *Proverbs, Sayings and Comparisons in Various Languages*. London. 1889.

O'Leary, C.F. *The World's Best Proverbs and Proverbial Phrases*. St. Louis. 1907.

Shearer, William. *Wisdom of the World in Proverbs*. New York. 1904.

Stanislawski, Jan. *English-Polish Dictionary*. McKay Company, Inc. New York.

Table of Contents

9   Love, Courtship, and Marriage

13   Historical View of Romance

14   Historic Proverbs

19   Law and Order

22   Religion

27   Home and Family

30   Bread and Beer

34   The Animal Kingdom

37   Nature

40   The Power of Money

45   Friends and Neighbors

50   Words of Wisdom

60   The Cycle of Life

Introduction

Just as an author's books are a key to his or her personality, a people's proverbs are a doorway to its culture's accumulated wisdom. Poles are gregarious, cheerful, hard-working, earnest people– these qualities are reflected in their proverbs. Many of these proverbs have been in existence for hundreds of years, and reflect, as well, traditional societal arrangements and relations with the natural world. But as much as they are Polish, these proverbs are also universal, each illuminating unchanging aspects of human nature with a few pithy words.

About Wycinanki

The art of paper cutting began to appear in Poland in the middle 1800s. In wycinanki, artists overlay different colors of paper, usually on a black silhouette, to create designs. Their work traditionally decorates country cottage walls, rafters, cupboards and windows, especially at Easter and Christmas. Springtime is reflected in the imagery of roosters, hens, birds, trees, and flowers.

As in the tradition of folk art, the designs are spontaneous, created as they are cut, and exude a fresh, non-labored appeal. The tool originally used was sheep shears, found in most farm homes. A variety of wycinanki styles are achieved through folding techniques (the paper can be folded many times, once, or not at all).

The Chinese invented the art of paper cutting and are known for using a sharp knife to create a stencil-type, block print image. In the *Polish Proverbs* book, the paper-cut artist has explored the positive and negative images of wycinanki as well as oriental stencil cutting.

Love, Courtship, and Marriage

Hope nourishes love.

Miłość karmi się nadzieją.

Every Adam will find his Eve.

What would Adam have done
   if the Lord
      did not create Eve?

With a bottle of wine
   and a pretty girl,
    one does not
       count the hours.

Neither advise nor dissuade
   from marriage,
     neither prevent nor force it.

Select a groom on horseback
   and a bride at a dance.

Beauty is the spice of virtue.

Love yourself, and
   be hated by the multitudes.

There are three things
that are difficult
to keep hidden:
a fire,
a cold,
and love.

One should live wildly for three years
    before marrying.

Love cannot exist
    without bread and salt.

**Love enters a man
    through his eyes and
      a woman through her ears.**

You cannot divide beauty
    into dollars.

Historical View
of Romance

Before going to war
    say one prayer,
     before going to sea say two,
before getting married
    say three prayers.

Historic Proverbs

All old times are good.

Wszystkie stare czasy są dobre.

A wife, a razor, and a horse
   are things that should not be lent.

A peasant's mouth can be stopped
   with bread.

Through bravery
   ## you may win a war,
      ## and through bravery
      ## you may lose.

Grass does not grow on a battlefield.

He that brandishes a sword
   will maintain the peace.

Peace does not last without conflict.

May the Lord
   ## grant me a sword
      ## and no need to use it.

The dog
that will bite you
growls,
the bee
that will sting you
hums,
but a girl will only make
her eyes smile.

─────── ○ 16 ○ ───────

The doorstep of the palace is slippery.

Krakow was not built in a day.

What the eyes do not see
the heart does not crave.

In Russia as one must,
in Poland as one will.

(Refers to the days when Russia had serfdom
and Poland did not.)

The children of a peasant
    are assets,
    the children of a gentleman
    are liabilities,
    the children of a nobleman
    are thieves.

Law and Order

Without work there is no bread.

Bez pracy nie ma kołaczy.

The thief takes only something,
the flame takes all.

Truth will not fill you,
nor will a lie choke you.

A liar can go around the world,
but cannot come back.

When the Lord blesses the harvest,
there is enough for the farmer
and the thief.

He who goes to court
over a hen
will have to make do
with an egg.

Nowadays to meet an angel,
you must go to Heaven.

Old truths, old laws,
old friends, an old book
and old wine
are best.

Religion

God gives nothing freely, but opens
everything, and everyone takes from
God as much as he wants.

Bóg nic darmo nie daje, lecz wszystko otwiera,
i każdy z Boga tyle, ile zechce, zabiera.

In church, at the inn and in the grave, all men are equal.

You would no doubt do little for the Lord if the devil were dead.

He who hasn't seen an altar bows before the stove.

If you are going to dine with the devil, take a long spoon.

The Lord will help a working man.

He who swims with the Lord will not sink beneath the waves.

The Lord gives to the one who rises early.

Trust in the Lord,
and then
put your shoulder
to the wheel.

What the Lord has given
    will not be taken away by jealousy.
What the Lord has not given
    will fall from your possession.

**The Lord has given all to all,
    and not all to one.**

A "God Bless You" does not buy much.

You should fear the Lord,
    and you should fear him
    who has no fear
        of the Lord.

If the Lord wills it,
even a rooster
can lay an egg.

Home and Family

The humblest cottage joyfully shares what it has.

Czem chata bogata, tem rada.

May our relatives prosper,
and may they never come visit.

A child is caressed by its mother,
an orphan is caressed
by God.

Mother's voice
is God's voice.

A guest in my home
        is God in my home.

Bread and Beer

A crust of bread and liberty.

Kęs chleba i swoboda.

Young beer is frothy.

Lower the sword
  and raise the glass!

Eat short banquets,
        live a long life.

If you can afford beer,
    drink water.
  If you can afford wine,
    drink beer.

It is a poor banquet without bread.

A good appetite
      needs no sauce.

The bread that is baked in the house
  should be eaten in the house.

Unless you have bread,
do not laugh
at poverty.

Without bread even meat has no flavor.

Bread cries
when eaten unearned.

You add salt to bread,
     not bread to salt.

He who has no bread
     should have no children.

If you have bread,
     do not look for cake as well.

The Animal Kingdom

The cock is the village clock.

The fatter the flea,
    the leaner the dog.

The skinny dog
    lives the longest.

Where one owl comes out,
    two others will soon follow.

Any goat can leap
    over a low wall.

He who sleeps
    with dogs
will wake up
    with fleas.

Every vixen praises her own tail.

He who buys a cage
will then want
a bird.

Nature

Wiser the egg than the hen.

Mądrzejsze jajo od kury.

The stars will twinkle at
        one the moon shines on.

There's no key
    to the woods and fields.

The night has its own code.

Everyone is willing to come
     and chop a fallen oak.

There is no rose without thorns.

Do not push the river;
    it will flow
      on its own accord.

If there is no wind,
    you must learn
      to row.

Spring is a maiden,
   summer a mother,
autumn a widow,
      and
   winter a stepmother.

The Power of Money

Rich is he who owes nothing.

Kto nie dłużny ten bogaty.

The man who lives in complete integrity
will have no shirt to wear.

The peasant's a born philosopher,
the aristocrat must
learn to be one.

Rich and poor alike agree
that it is better to wear out the feet
than the boots.

If you are born for the cap,
do not wish for the crown.

Misfortune comes on horseback
and departs on foot.

The rich man and the poor man
both have two ears.

The rich don't know themselves,
and no one knows the poor.

Where the peasant
is poor,
the entire country
is poor.

The poor are cured by
    hard work and sweat;
    the rich are cured by the doctor.

Walk slowly and poverty
    will overtake you;
    walk quickly and
    you will catch up with it.

To the hard-working poor,
    even the wedding night is short.

For the poor it is always dark
    and always winter.

The poor always have the wind
    in their faces as they walk uphill.

He who is satisfied
with little
is not so poor
as he who
never has enough.

Friends and Neighbors

Love your neighbor,
but do not remove the fence.

Kochaj swego sąsiada, ale nie usuwaj płota.

The field held in common is always
ravaged by the wind.

A guest sees more in an hour
than the host
in a year.

He who seems always kind
may not be kind always.

What you give
to a good friend
is not lost.

When misfortune knocks at the door,
friends are sound asleep.

He who says good-bye
with tears in his eyes,
will greet you with joy.

He who gives
        should forget;
he who takes
        should remember
                forever.

An old shoe
    and an old friend
        are the most dear.

Let him who has deliberately
    walked into the mire
        walk out by himself.

A man's friends are thieves of his time.

That which is guarded
    by everyone
        will soon disappear.

One who hates his neighbors
    will even find blame in the heavens.

He who lends money
    to a friend makes an enemy.

Friendship is like wine—
the older it is,
the better it is.

Words of Wisdom

He who gives freely gives twice.

Kto prędko daje, dwa razy daje.

A good painter does not have to
give his painting a name;
a bad painter must.

A noisy cow gives little milk;
great talkers are little doers.

The one absent is always to blame.

Only what I think
is truly mine.

Even a spoiled apple is eaten by worms.

He who asks without confidence
asks to be refused.

Better an ounce of luck
than a pound of gold.

Hold tight to the first bargain.

Bargaining teaches us
how to buy.

The one who blames himself,
praises himself.

He who waits for another's shoes
will walk around barefoot.

Every bubble bursts.

He who attains greatness
is immediately changed.

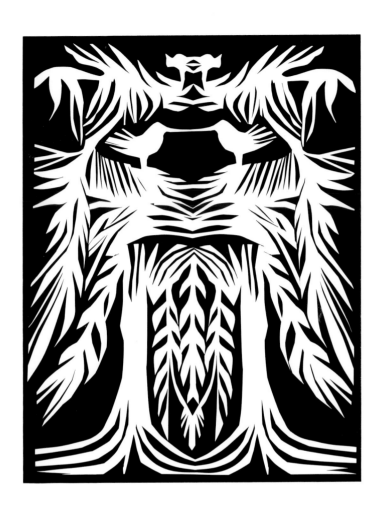

The roots of learning
are bitter,
but the fruit
is sweet.

Word of a good deed
travels far,
word of a bad deed
even farther.

Every error has its own excuse.

Carefully watch the face of the one
who bows low before you.

If you are feared by many,
be afraid of many.

Everyone will get in
where the fence is low.

There is a Sunday in every week,
but there is also a Friday.
(Refers to the no meat on Friday rule.)

Forgive others easily,
but do not forgive yourself.

Even a pin is worth
bending down for.

To believe
with certainty,
we must begin
with doubting.

Put in a good word for a bad girl;
for a good girl you may
say what you like.

The tavern will not spoil
the virtuous,
nor a church improve
the wicked.

For every fool
there are two more.

To accept a favor is to lose
your freedom.

He who is worth anything
is spoken about.

Gratitude has gone to heaven
and has taken the ladder.

Dirt stains your hands only
　　if you touch it.

He who has been locked out
　　of the main gate must knock
　　　on the side entrance.

It is better not to begin than,
　　having begun,
　　　　to leave unfinished.

A good listener
makes a
good teacher.

The Cycle of Life

As one makes his bed,
so must he lie in it.

Jak sobie kto pościele, tak się wyśpi.

The gallows and the cross
    are both made of wood.

The mistakes of the doctor
        are covered by the earth.

The young may die, the old will.

It hurts more when
    no one knows
        about the pain.

He who cries during life dies smiling.

When death is near,
    repentance is not difficult.

The more one sleeps,
        the less one lives.

Wherever you go,
     you can never leave
          yourself behind.

A dead man's will is
          the mirror of his life.

Life is like the moon—
     now dark,
          now full.

To whom life
        was heavy,
    the earth
        is light.

Proverbs are the wisdom of the people.

Przysłowia są mądrością narodu.